Road Warrior Blues

☐ Are on the road at least one quarter of the year.

☐ Cram a week's worth of clothes and accessories into the standard rollie bag.

☐ Have no control over transportation delays – flights and trains, traffic.

☐ Go long stretches without food.

☐ Arrive at your hotel either too early or too late to have a normal meal.

☐ Are away from family, friends and routine.

☐ Are constantly stressed. More emails and conference calls "after hours," another business dinner. Incredibly long work days that can easily exceed 12-15 hours a day.

RESULT:

With all of this disruption, eating healthy on the road often feels like a losing battle. Life up in the air, on the ground and constant stress are all recipes for terrible food choices.

But there is hope.

TRAVEL HEALTHY:
A Road Warrior's Guide to Eating Healthy

NATASHA LEGER

Blue Pearl Media, LLC

TRAVEL HEALTHY:
A ROAD WARRIOR'S GUIDE TO EATING HEALTHY

Copyright ©2013 by Natasha Léger

The author has made every effort to provide accurate links and Internet addresses at the time of publication. Neither the publisher nor the author assume any responsibility for errors or for changes that occur after publication.

Blue Pearl Media books may be ordered through booksellers or by contacting bluepearl-media.com

Illustrations, including the cover by Andrew Sternard

ISBN (paperback)
978-0-9912465-0-2

ISBN (pdf)
978-0-9912465-1-9

Printed in the United States on sustainability certified paper.

www.travelhealthybook.com

DEDICATION

I dedicate this book to Annapurna, the Hindu Goddess of Nourishment
within all of us, to my mother who taught me to have the courage to break the cycle in
any relationship that is no longer working, and to Téah Mantzke, a ten year old beacon of
light who passed away from brain cancer April 6, 2013.

ACKNOWLEDGEMENTS

Craig Bachmann
for his never-ending support and always
challenging me to strive higher and higher.
This book would not have been possible without him.

Nadya Peeva and Marlene Ziobrowski
for their attention to detail and copy editing skills.

Myrna James Yoo
for teaching me the art of publishing
and for leaving her fingerprints on this book.

Natalie Cutsforth, John Daharsh, and Dorothy Orszulak
for taking the time out of their busy schedules to read the manuscript.
Their unique perspectives have made this a better book.

John Wagner
for sharing his hotel management experience and perspective.

Andrew Sternard,
graphic designer extraordinaire for his incredible talent,
translating my vision, and being such a delightful person.

Cynthia Williams, who inspired me to write this book.

Lastly, to my fellow road warriors, and many friends, colleagues, and acquaintences
who have expressed frustration with the modern work environment and the impact
it is having on their health: I feel your pain. I have written this book for you and
others experiencing that same frustration.

This is not a diet book.

Diets are rigid, unsustainable and frankly unhealthy.

This book is about *You* and the challenges of business travel.

THIS GUIDEBOOK WILL HELP YOU MAKE FOOD CHOICES
WHILE TRAVELING INCLUDING:

→ Committing to a "healthy" relationship with food and your body

→ Deciding to eat what will nourish your cells and boost your immune system, and

→ Choosing when something is worth the damage and compensating for it later.

CONFERENCE FOOD?

HOTEL RESTAURANT?

COFFEE SHOP?

AIRPORT FOOD?

TABLE OF CONTENTS

FIGURES & TABLES

PREFACE

I travel approximately one-quarter of the year both domestically and internationally. I know many of you consider airplane Seat 2B, or your Business Class or Economy "Plus" seat (when you frequent flyers do not get the upgrade) home, given the amount of time you spend in it. We are all different, and have different relationships with food as a result of body types, culture, personalities, and even stress. Yet, we all struggle with finding good and healthy food while traveling, especially when traveling on business.

Many people have asked me over the years how I stay healthy on the road. A new acquaintance at a recent business dinner inspired me to write this book. She mentioned that despite all the websites, books and videos on how to develop a healthy lifestyle and healthy eating habits, nothing made anything easy for business travelers. In particular, most of the recommendations in these resources are all around how to prepare your own meals at home. But what happens when extensive business travel turns the whole notion of "home" upside down? What happens to your food choices when so much is outside your control, or at least appears to be?

Health and diet books are often overwhelming. They can also be discouraging if you feel like you cannot stick to their plans. I have synthesized over 15 years of research and experience into a practical guidebook. Being healthy and eating healthy on the road is really simple if you put your mind to it. You are not a victim of the travel environment. You just need to feel and know that you have choices.

I am going to share with you some tricks and approaches that I have learned over the years. They are by no means exhaustive, but I hope that they can inspire you to avoid despair in situations that may often appear to offer no options.

But first, it is important to understand and acknowledge that being healthy is a function of five variables:

1. The food you eat (and drink);

2. The amount of movement your body gets;

3. The environment in which you live and work;

4. Your emotions; and

5. How well you manage stress.

BALANCING ALL FIVE WHILE ON THE ROAD CAN OFTEN BE A CHALLENGE.

This book addresses the eating part of staying healthy on the road. Exercise, environment and stress management components will be the subject of another book. However, there are some things you should always keep in mind.

1. The body wants to be in a constant state of motion. Always try to optimize your movement. For example, walk the length of the airport terminal, train, bus, or ferry station; explore on foot the neighborhood in which your hotel is located.

2. To the extent you have control over where you stay, you should opt for places where you can explore on foot. Business parks are by far the most challenging in regards to supporting a healthy lifestyle and finding nouri (healthy food). They are often far from a city center, lack a grocery store nearby, and surrounded by corporate hotels, and restaurant chains (fast food and casual dining) that often provide limited nouri options. They are especially challenging when you find yourself in a business park in a foreign country and you do not speak the language. If you are not a runner, and you manage to fit exercise clothes and shoes into your rollie, try to take advantage of the gym facilities provided by your hotel.

While this book is focused on eating healthy on the road, and the challenges and limitations that come with business travel, much of it is applicable to when you are home. The choices you make (and the habits you change) are a function of the options available to you in a particular environment. Your food options at home are much different from those available at the airport, at a hotel, at a conference center, or at the office. Options change with the company you keep; vegetarians vs. carnivores, foodies vs. convenience food seekers, people who see food as pleasure vs. those who see food as fuel or a scheduled meal, and people who see breakfast, lunch and dinner meetings as an obligation vs. an opportunity. They also change based on geographically influenced culinary preferences–New Orleans vs. Boston vs. Paris vs. London. Accepting and understanding these differences is the first step to making informed choices.

According to the National Restaurant Association, 47% of every food dollar is spent dining out. This is the equivalent of $2,620 in average household food expenditure spent on food away from home. With nearly 50% of meals eaten at restaurants where you have no idea of what is really in the food you are eating, how can frequent diners be healthy?

Here is another statistic for you. Every $1 spent on bad food results in $5 spent on healthcare. The healthcare costs include treatments for chronic diseases and over-the-counter and prescription drugs that can amount to hundreds or thousands of dollars per month depending on the situation. Many people also spend between $20- $100 per month on vitamins and supplements. Therefore food choices should not be seen as short-term, no-impact decisions. In other words, you can pay for it now or pay for it later. You can pay for the food or pay for the doctor and prescription drugs... but the doctor and drug combo is guaranteed to be more expensive.

THE SECRET to making wise food choices is understanding food–what it is, and how it works in the body. This book is about how to think about your food choices so you can empower yourself, take control of what you eat, and listen to your body.

This book is intended for people who are currently not suffering from any particular ailments but realize that they are not eating as healthy as they could while traveling. It does not address specific diets required to manage celiac, cardiovascular, diabetes, or other diseases. The book starts with some context around why eating healthy on the road is a challenge, including the business models behind restaurants and food establishments. It then proceeds to define what is healthy and unhealthy, illustrate various travel scenarios, and explain how to think through options in a particular scenario. It concludes with suggestions on using corporate budgets and power to influence the food options provided by restaurants, hotels, conference centers, and airport, train, bus and ferry terminals.

INTRODUCTION

The Road Warrior life is anything but glamorous. It is a constant struggle from home to the airport or train station to hotel and meetings. The movie *Up in the Air* was a little too close to home for many of us – down to the 35 minutes saved by not checking your bags. Cram a week's worth of clothes and accessories into the standard rollie bag. Delayed flights and trains, traffic. Long stretches without food. Arrive at your hotel either too early or too late. Away from family, friends and routine. Stressed. More emails and conference calls, another business dinner. With all of this disruption, eating healthy on the road often feels like a losing battle. Life up in the air, on the ground and constant stress are all recipes for terrible food choices.

Eating on the road is not easy, especially with today's current industrial food supply and food services market. Work commitments and time scarcity add to the challenge. But it can be done. It is possible to make healthy choices; it just takes a little discipline, a new perspective, a commitment to conscious eating, and an appreciation for moderation.

Think of this book as a guidebook, or a companion you can turn to when you find yourself in a challenging or unhealthy food environment. Unlike many other health and diet books out there, I am not going to tell you what you need to deprive yourself of to be healthy. Instead, I am going to help you think about how you can proactively contribute to your health with your food choices, especially in challenging situations.

It all starts with changing your vocabulary.

A PRACTICAL AND PROACTIVE APPROACH TO EATING HEALTHY

A little about me before we begin...

The majority of books on healthy living and diets begin with stories of how the authors were overweight, or hit the wall because they were diagnosed with some awful disease, which forced them to change their lifestyle. That is not me. I changed my eating habits and lifestyle because I was tired of feeling tired, and something just did not feel right.

I was raised under a tight food budget. We ate lots of canned and packaged foods, but my Mom was obsessed about vitamins. I didn't really like vegetables at that time, but loved fruits. I drank a lot of Classic Coke, and ate Doritos and Frosted Flakes. (I really cringe at the thought now—and that was before genetically modified organisms [GMO's] and the use of antibiotics and hormones in the food supply). My first year in college, I lived on bagels and turkey sandwiches because the dormitory food was so bad. I studied abroad in Singapore and Thailand for 6 months and ate fresh food and lots of veggies and fruits. I returned twenty pounds lighter.

I started drinking coffee when I got to law school, and that's when I started officially working out at a gym. I can't say I had any health problems at the time, but I certainly was not healthy because I was not eating foods that positively impacted my cells.

I started juicing in 1997 when I found a $20 juicer on sale at Macy's. I started reading about detoxing, and all the toxins that accumulate in the body from bad food, caffeine and the environment around us. I stopped drinking coffee, abandoned my afternoon latte breaks, but still kept eating the same way.

Two years later I moved back to New York and undertook a high stress job that resulted in working about 16 hours a day. I could not make it through the day without coffee, so I got back on the drug. I had a one hour train commute that first year, and always knew what day of the week it was by how far I got through reading the newspaper on the morning ride. Monday I would get through the whole New York Times, Tuesday, three-quarters, Wednesday half, Thursday one quarter, and Friday I would be out cold. I would work out in the morning, then work straight through the day. Lunch was ordered in every day, and at least three times a week I would eat dinner at the office. At the time eating out all the time and being taken home by a car service seemed like a glamourous lifestyle.

One night, about two years into this job, I went home feeling like an absolute toxic waste product. I was tired of always feeling tired, depending on stimulants like coffee to perk me up (which then of course caused me to crash and put me into a vicious cycle of regular lattes a day), and looking forward to wine or brandy to decompress when I got home at night. I opened a juicing book, flipped to the cleansing pages and decided that night to do a cleanse. I embarked on a three week cleanse which changed my relation-ship with food.

I did not follow this cleanse religiously, but along with taking betonite clay and psyllium husk twice a day for three weeks, I eliminated sugar, caffeine, alcohol, meat (although I did still eat fish and chicken occasionally) and processed foods from my diet. Ideally this cleanse is done on a raw foods diet, so I cheated a bit...but it worked. All I can say is that after the three weeks I felt more energized and clean from the inside out! I started becoming more conscious of my food intake. I stuck to the same "diet" after the cleanse.

A few months later, it was time to shop for Thanksgiving dinner. When I looked down at the grocery cart I noticed something different. All the items, with the exception of the canned tomatoes, were all fresh! There were no processed or packaged foods in my cart. I soon abandoned canned tomatoes a few months later. Have you ever noticed that, unlike fresh tomatoes, canned tomatoes don't melt when you cook them?

Ever since, my relationship with food has been about making choices that make me feel better – eating foods that don't make me feel tired, bloated, or sluggish. Eating foods that are easy (low impact) on the body. I stopped drinking coffee and alcohol. I did not set out to become a vegetarian, but turned into one, with the exception of occasional fish consumption. I found that after eating fish I felt sluggish and lethargic. I err on the side of raw foods (fruits, vegetables, nuts and seeds) and slow cooking of foods that are easy for the body to digest and result in optimum bio-availability of nutrients. I am a nouri seeker. More on nouri later.

I run a consulting company, am editor of a location intelligence magazine, recently co-founded a non-profit industry association, and am in the process of developing a digital service for the yoga community. I work between 10-16 hours a day, depending on the day, and still make time to make fresh juice every morning when I'm home, make home-cooked meals, and practice yoga. It can be done! When I'm on the road, I always think in terms of first "where can I find nouri?" and second, in the absence of nouri, "is it worth the damage?"

Welcome to a Road Warrior's Guide to Eating Healthy.

THE PROBLEM: WHY IS EATING HEALTHY ON THE ROAD SUCH A CHALLENGE?

Business travel inevitably means time-scarcity induced stress—rushing to the airport or meeting, day long meetings and presentations, delayed flights or trains, and more. This environment alone puts stress on your eating choices of when to eat, how much time you have to eat, and where to eat. While your time may feel out of your control when on business travel, food itself appears to be out of your control for three main reasons:

✈ NUTRITIONAL FACT:
Eating healthy is not just about counting calories and managing the intake of sugar, salt, and fats. Instead it is all about the nutrient value of food. Unfortunately, most of the food we encounter on the road (and all processed food) is devoid of nutrients.

✈ YOUR PERSPECTIVE:
So much feels outside of your control when you are traveling. When eating at restaurants or consuming packaged and prepared foods you really don't know the source of the ingredients and how the food was prepared.

✈ FOOD SERVICE BUSINESS REALITY:
The definition of food quality and the business incentives and constraints of food service providers ultimately determine the majority of food options presented to you.

Food Options Drivers

FOOD QUALITY STANDARDS

Food quality, instead of being associated with nutrient value, is often associated with:

- consumer expectations of quality, such as appearance (size, shape, color, gloss, and consistency), texture, and flavor;
- factors such as federal food grade standards for commodity products such as eggs, meat and poultry; and
- use of pesticides and chemicals.

Food quality is generally not associated with the nutrient value of the food, which is affected by the way the food is grown, transported, processed, and prepared.

FOOD SERVICE BUSINESS

- Airport and train station restaurants and food services focus on selling convenience foods that can be easily stored, shipped, and have long shelf-lives. These foods are generally heavily processed, and full of salt, sugar. Fast food chains generally serve foods that are fried, high in fat, salt, and sugar.
- Airlines continue to cut costs and only offer commodity products. On long-haul flights, the food served is packaged convenience food and the equivalent of TV dinners.
- Many restaurant owners, especially restaurant chains, sacrifice the nutrient quality of food for cost advantages. Most people in the food business,

Figure 1

unfortunately very much like doctors,[1] have not been trained in nutrition. As a result, they often do not understand the connection between food and a healthy body and consequently do not even know they may be selling foods that contribute to long-term illness.

→ Restaurants are in the business of managing food inventory and minimizing the costs associated with perishability. Nonetheless, every day there are more restaurant owners starting to question what they are really serving and changing their food supply. This has become known as **the farm-to-table movement.**

→ Food service distributors like Sysco, which supply restaurants with food products, have systems in place, along with high insurance liability requirements, that discourage and even prevent sourcing from small local farms that produce higher nutrient quality food than factory farms and large corporate farms (even when the restaurants request it).[2]

HOTELS AND CONFERENCE CENTERS

→ Room service menus in hotels try to appeal to as many people as possible, and therefore offer a wide variety of options. However the options tend to lean towards the tasteless and the unhealthy.

→ Conference organizers determine the menu for coffee breaks, lunch, and appetizers for networking events. Decisions are generally based on price and the types of foods that make it easier to encourage networking (think wraps and finger foods instead of salad).

→ Business parks often do not have restaurants or grocery stores within walking distance.

---

1 Although this is starting to change within a small segment of the medical profession, the role of diet in well being has been a taboo subject in Western medicine, especially in the United States. Medical schools do not focus on nutrition.
2 See Joel Salatin, *Folks, This Ain't Normal,* for a farmer's perspective on supplying the restaurant market.

This leaves the road warrior to fend for herself in an environment that is currently not set up to optimize health. But all that can change...

FOOD RULES

RULE 1: VISION
Just because you *CAN* doesn't mean you *SHOULD.*

Before you order food, put something on your plate, or take a bite... ask yourself:

✈ Is this going to positively impact my health?

✈ Is this going to negatively impact my health? If so, is it worth the damage?

✈ Can I compensate for or recover from any negative impacts of my food choice today?

RULE 2: RETURN ON INVESTMENT
No one is going to take care of you except for you. Bottom Line.

RULE 3: RETURN ON ASSET
The human body—your body—is AMAZING and should be treated as if your life depends on it. Because it does.

RULE 4: RESPONSIBILITY
You control what you eat and what you drink. Don't be a victim.

RULE 5: OUTLOOK
Healthy is not a trend; it is an attitude and a lifestyle.

Now that you know the five rules, apply them within the context of your food reality...

Food Realities

1. 90% of food and beverages available in grocery stores and restaurants have nothing to do with what is good for you. Instead, is the result of shelf life, the low cost to produce, transport and distribute, convenience, and getting you to part with your money for what you think is food that will sustain or nourish you.

2. The majority of chefs, unfortunately like doctors, are not trained in nutrition. While most chefs recognize that the fresher the ingredients, the better tasting the food, the real question is how they prepare those fresh ingredients. Chefs are trained in altering the molecular structure of foods to achieve certain taste and texture preferences. This involves adding heat and mixing ingredients that may or may not result in a healthy outcome... albeit tasty.

3. Nouri, as described on page 16, is currently a niche market. It is available but you need to make an effort to find it and choose it.

Current Vocabulary

FOOD *noun.* Any nourishing substance that is eaten, drunk, or otherwise taken into the body to sustain life, provide energy, promote growth, etc.

NUTRIMENT *noun.* Something that nourishes; food.

NOURISHMENT *noun.* Something that nourishes; food; sustenance.

NOURISH *verb.* To sustain with food or nutriment; to strengthen or promote.

NUTRIENT *adjective.* Nourishing; providing nourishment or nutriment.

NONE OF THESE WORDS REALLY CAPTURE THE VITAL ROLE THAT FOOD PLAYS IN OUR HEALTH. Partly because food itself is not well defined, at least from the perspective of what constitutes the promotion of good health.

HEALTH *noun.* The general condition of the body or mind with reference to soundness or vigor. Freedom from disease or ailment.

HEALTHY *adj.* 1. possessing or enjoying good health or a sound and vigorous mentality. 2. pertaining to or characteristic of good health, or a sound and vigorous mind.

Change the Word, Change Your Perspective

Let's all adopt a new word to reflect the real meaning of food in our lives and our health...

NOURI *noun.* Any plant or animal based protein, fat, carbohydrate, vitamin, mineral, or phytonutrient, that is ingested in liquid or solid form, that improves the cellular functions of the body to strengthen the immune system, promote energy, and reduce the risk of illness or disease. Nouri is food that has high nutrient value that benefits the body.

Don't Look for Food, Look for *Nouri!*

Food Rules + Realities =
~~Food~~ Nouri Choice

THIS IS A BOOK ABOUT MAKING CHOICES.

What does being and eating *healthy* really mean, and more importantly what does it mean to you?

The only way to commit to eating healthy, and even defining **healthy**, is to first understand what is **unhealthy**. More precisely, in defining healthy and unhealthy, we want to understand what the impact of consuming these foods are on the body and to you specifically.

Your Body's Key Performance Indicators When it Comes to Food

The longest and most intimate relationship you will ever have is with your body. Curiously enough, many of us know very little about our bodies. In fact we often know more about abstract things and useless trivia than we do about the body that keeps us alive and protects us from the elements.[1] So it is time to get personal with your body. The human body is an amazing and complex piece of biological engineering. However, when it comes to eating, the two most important things you need know about your body are:

→ **YOUR LIVER, GALL BLADDER, AND KIDNEYS ARE YOUR WASTE MANAGEMENT SYSTEM.** If they get over-taxed or clogged they don't work properly and result in poor metabolism. When the body does not properly metabolize foods, nutrients are not absorbed by cells and cells begin to mutate or die. In addition, toxins overflow into the bloodstream that lead to illness.

→ **YOUR INTESTINAL TRACT (GUT) IS YOUR WASTE TRANSIT SYSTEM.** If your intestinal walls become porous (leaky gut) undigested foods make their way directly into your bloodstream and cause a chain reaction of immune responses that cause illness. When this occurs your body basically goes into defense mode against the constant onslaught of invaders. The body cannot sustain this long-term defense so it breaks down in the form of illness and disease.

If the traffic in your intestinal tract gets backed up, pollution accumulates. The build up of this intestinal pollution breeds disease.

WHEN THE WASTE MANAGEMENT AND TRANSIT SYSTEMS DO NOT WORK PROPERLY:

1. nutrients are not absorbed (often called poor metabolism); and

2. toxins overflow into the bloodstream which causes illness or disease.

1. The all-important mind, body, spirit connection that works in concert to keep us in an optimum state of health and well being is the subject of many other books.

Food Impact: Unhealthy

You really want to understand the impact of food on your liver, gall bladder, kidneys, and intestinal tract. I like to think in terms of low and high impact foods. Low impact foods do not require the body to work hard to process them. When the body can easily process foods, the liver, gall bladder, kidneys and intestinal tract function optimally. High impact foods, on the other hand, require the body to work a lot harder, requiring more energy, and the production of enzymes to process foods. When the body can't process these foods, the liver, gall bladder, kidneys and intestinal tract are over-taxed and can no longer serve their purpose.

WHAT IS UNHEALTHY FOOD?

Simply, unhealthy foods are those foods that negatively impact proper cell functions and metabolism. These types of foods slow down the body's systems and force it to compensate in ways that manifest in illness. ***These are high impact foods.***

More specifically, an unhealthy diet fails to supply the essential nutrients your body needs in order to function properly. Adverse effects on the body include producing symptoms of deficiency, disease and improper weight. Your body needs dozens of proteins, carbohydrates, fatty acids, vitamins and minerals to sustain life. Consistently eating unhealthy foods can reduce your levels of essential nutrients such as iron, calcium, vitamin C or any of the seven B vitamins. A nutritional imbalance can come from eating mostly processed foods, factory-farm and factory-fed animal products including meats and dairy that are high in hormones, antibiotics, and GMO feed, pesticide-contaminated foods, and refined sugars.[2]

2. Read more: http://www.livestrong.com/article/401518-definition-of-an-unhealthy-diet/#ixzz209B1mJmr

The following foods are considered to be high impact and unhealthy because they contribute to weight gain, destroy healthy cells, or slow down metabolic processes, which overtaxes the body's waste management system—its natural ability to eliminate toxins.

SUGARS:

→ The human body only needs 2 teaspoons of sugar, obtained from digestion of complex carbohydrates, protein and fat, at any one time for proper metabolic functioning. Consuming large amounts of refined sugar, artificial sweeteners, and high fructose corn syrup (HFCS) puts unnecessary stress on the body that leads to inflammation and disease; not to mention weight gain.

→ Refined sugar, such as white sugar, causes inflammation in the body. "Refined sugar is, in fact, nutrientless. Important nutrients such as chromium, manganese, cobalt, copper, zinc, and magnesium are stripped away in sugar refining, and our bodies actually have to use their own mineral reserves just to digest it."[3]

→ Artificial sweeteners:

- Aspartame (known as Equal or NutraSweet, and e951 food additive in the European Union [EU]) depletes the bodies' supplies of chromium which is important in sugar metabolism. It also suppresses the production of serotonin, a neurotransmitter that regulates food cravings. Aspartame, while sugar free and zero calories, causes weight gain.

- Sucrolose (known as Splenda, and as e955 food additive in the EU) is made by chlorinating table sugar. The body does not breakdown sucrolose.

- Saccharin (known as Sweet'n Low) is a petroleum derivative which has been banned in several countries over the years.

3. For more than you ever wanted to know about sugar read Ann Louise Gittleman's *Get the Sugar Out: 501 Simple Ways to Cut the Sugar Out of Any Diet*

→ High fructose corn syrup (HFCS): The body is not designed to metabolize HFCS. Since the body doesn't recognize HFCS it doesn't know how to process it or control it, which means that it becomes stored fat. HFCS is found in about every processed food including sodas, juices, candies, syrups, pasta sauces, cookies, cakes, energy bars, baked goods, canned foods, salad dressing, breakfast cereals, yogurt, ketchup, frozen foods, baby formula, and more. If you are buying packaged foods and snacks, read labels carefully to avoid this toxin. If you are dining out at restaurants, whether fine dining, or fast food, be aware of what might sabotage a seemingly healthy looking meal.

CAFFEINE:

This stimulant induces a roller coaster effect of high and low energy. It is often consumed in the form of coffee, tea, and soft drinks. Caffeine has a few notable negative impacts on the body.

1. It can contribute to weight gain depending on the amount of consumption and the other ingredients that make up the caffeinated product. High intake of caffeine increases stress levels which leads to hunger and sugar cravings, and affects fat storage in the body. Coffee, soft drinks, tea, and chocolate that contain high calorie, fat, or sugar ingredients contribute to weight gain.

2. Caffeine pulls calcium from the bone, flushing needed calcium out of the body.

PROCESSED FOODS:

When food is processed and heated (pasteurized) the original nutritional value of the whole food is lost. It also takes on a different molecular structure which the body is not set up to handle. This new chemistry puts a lot of stress on the body because the body has to create digestive enzymes to break down the food. This means that any nutrients left in the food are not easily absorbed by the body (this equals no nouri gain). Processed foods often act as toxins, causing the body to develop an immune response that results in symptoms of illness such as allergies, obesity, joint pain, and more. In addition, the majority of processed foods today are made with high fructose corn syrup which results in excess fat storage.

GMO FOODS:

A GMO (genetically modified organism) is the result of a laboratory process of taking genes from one species and inserting them into another in an attempt to obtain a desired trait or characteristic; hence they are also known as transgenic organisms. This process may be called either Genetic Engineering (GE) or Genetic Modification (GM); they are one and the same. The safety of GMOs has not been proven over the long term. Instead, current laboratory tests have proven that GMO-fed lab animals develop cancer and other illnesses, including infertility, immune problems and accelerated aging. GMO foods leave genetically modified bacteria in the gut that can change the DNA of cells resulting in a number of ailments.[4] See list of top GMO-based food products in the Appendix.

ANIMAL PRODUCTS:

Studies have shown that drinking hormone-laced milk causes tumors in laboratory animals. Eating pasteurized dairy products such as cheese and yogurt, and eating meat from animals pumped with antibiotics fosters an antibiotic resistant environment within your body. In addition, eating meat from animals fed a grain diet makes you more susceptible to disease. Grain-fed animal meat is as acidic as human stomach acid. The result is bacteria that survive in the animal's gut, which are toxic to humans, can now survive in the human gut. Our stomach acid can no longer kill off this bad bacteria. Several studies have correlated cancer with diets that exceed 5% in animal protein (organic or otherwise). The most extensive study conducted on the impact of diet on health is *The China Study* by T. Colin Campbell and Thomas M. Campbell, II. Processed meats also contain the preservative sodium nitrate which is a known carcinogen. (The USDA even tried to ban it in the 1970s but was vetoed by the food industry.)

4. See Institute for Responsible Technology for more information on GMOs. The Center for Food Safety published *True Food Shopper's Guide: How to Avoid Foods Made with Genetically Modified Organisms (GMOs) in 2011*. This guide was also turned into an iPhone and Android app called True Food. WholeFoods admitted in 2012 that many of their organic-labelled products contained GMO ingredients. While True Food Shopper's Guide is not perfect, it is a good start in knowing more about your food and brands.

CHEMICALLY TREATED FOODS:

Chemicals such as pesticides, fungicides, and fertilizers never get washed away from foods, even when cooked. When ingested these chemicals weaken and destroy your cells over time, which causes disease.

WHEAT:

Wheat production has changed in the last fifty years. Wheat strains have been hybridized, crossbred, and introgressed to make the wheat plant resistant to environmental conditions, such as drought, or pathogens such as fungi. But most of all, genetic changes have been induced to increase yield per acre. The biochemical differences between these man-made strains of wheat have resulted in small changes to the wheat protein structure can induce a devastating immune response. Regular consumption of modern day wheat products triggers an insulin response, which results in fat storage, which creates inflammation in the body that leads to a number of ailments.[5]

REFINED GRAINS:

Refined grains are crushed, which destroys the bran, which is the outer protective coating of the grain, and the germ, which is loaded with vitamins and minerals.[6]

---

5. See *Wheat Belly* by William Davis for the history of wheat adulteration and how it works in the body.

6. Read more: http://www.livestrong.com/article/28448-example-grain-foods/#ixzz2PFYGEDZ5

TABLE **1**

Do you know if what you are eating is unhealthy?
Does your diet primarily consist of:

FOOD CATEGORY	AS IT MAY APPEAR ON A MENU
☐ Dead foods (cooked at high temperatures, microwaved)	☐ Baked, broiled, barbecued, roasted, boiled, fried, steamed
☐ Refined grains	☐ Corn tortillas, crackers, white and wheat breads, pastas, and most baked sweets.
☐ Refined sugars	☐ Table sugar, cookies, pastries, breads, pancake syrup.
☐ Genetically modified (GM) foods, such as corn, soy, and sugar from GM sugar beets	☐ Edamame, cornbread, tofu, croissants, pastries
☐ Hormone-laden and pasteurized conventional dairy products, such as cow's milk	☐ Cheese, yogurt, cream, milk, ice cream
☐ Foods made with hundreds of different chemical food additives, from MSG and aspartame to chemical preservatives	☐ Soft drinks, chips, cereal, soups, sauces

FOOD CATEGORY	AS IT MAY APPEAR ON A MENU
☐ Conventionally grown pesticide contaminated foods	☐ Strawberries/berries, apples, orange juice, apple juice, bananas, corn, potatoes, tomatoes, melons, etc.
☐ Large quantity of unhealthy oils	☐ Corn, soy, canola, vegetable or partially hydrogenated oils
☐ Large number of fried foods	☐ Deep fried, batter fried, chicken, fish, french fries, onion rings, potato chips, falafels, egg rolls
☐ Factory-farmed or factory-fed animal products	☐ Chicken nuggets, ground beef/ hamburger, chicken breasts, steak, beef stew, pork, ham, roast beef, pastrami, sausage, meatballs, farm-raised shrimp and fish, turkey

Are You Unhealthy?

☐ Do you have chronic pain?

☐ Are you moody?

☐ Do you have high medical bills?

☐ Are you easily injured?

☐ Do you get sick often?

☐ Do you have reproductive disorders?

☐ Do you have difficulty sleeping?

☐ Do others find you to be irritable or unpleasant?

☐ Is your weight management out of control?

☐ Do you have gastro-intestinal disorders?

☐ Do you have skin disorders?

☐ Do you rely on stimulants, over-the-counter or prescription drugs?

If you checked any of the above categories, you should look closely at your food choices, and determine if they are really worth the damage.

Figure 2

**Unhealthy Food Impact on the Body:
Is It Worth the Damage?**

	WEIGHT GAIN	DESTROY HEALTHY CELLS	SLOW DOWN METABOLIC PROCESSES
Sugars –Refined sugar –Artificial sweeteners –High Fructose Corn Syrup	✓	✓	✓
Caffeine	✓	✓	✓
Processed Foods	✓	✓	✓
GMO Foods	✓	✓	✓
Animal Products		✓	✓
Chemically Treated Foods		✓	✓
Wheat (modern hybridized strain)	✓	✓	✓

Now that you know what is unhealthy, what is defined as health and healthy?

PERHAPS MORE IMPORTANTLY IS DETERMINING WHAT
BEING AND EATING HEALTHY MEANS TO YOU.

Food Impact: Nouri (Healthy)

Nouri, let alone healthy, is not defined by the health marketing labels on a package, or calories per meal. It is important to read labels and menu descriptions, but there is more to eating healthy than eating something that is labeled fat free, sugar free, low carb, low salt, etc.

Many diet books and sports nutritionists advocate monitoring calories. However, the problem with counting calories is that it has nothing to do with nutrients.

Eating healthy means consuming foods that provide vital nutrients to your cells, are easily digestible and do not over-tax your body (low impact foods), especially your liver, gall bladder, and kidneys, and do not damage your cells or DNA. **Think nouri, not food!**

The positive impact of nouri on your body includes improved cellular function, rejuvenation of cells, maintenance or improvement of metabolic functions, maintenance of optimum weight, and increased energy. The consumption of various types of nouri work together to form a symphony of health.

Nouri

noun. Any plant or animal based protein, fat, carbohydrate, vitamin, or mineral, or phytonutrient, that is ingested in liquid or solid form, that improves the cellular functions of the body to strengthen the immune system, promote energy, and reduce the risk of illness or disease. Nouri is food that has high nutrient value that benefits the body.

The following foods are considered to be low impact and healthy (nouri) because they are easily digestible, high in nutrients, and do not over-tax the body.

ORGANIC AND GMO-FREE FOODS:

✦ Fresh, chemical-free, non-GMO whole fruits and vegetables.

- Fruits: apples, berries (strawberries, blueberries, blackberries, raspberries), oranges, pineapple, melons, grapes, bananas, plums, kiwis, papaya, and more.

- Vegetables: carrots, beets, broccoli, cauliflower, potatoes, squash, mushrooms, tomatoes (technically a fruit), beans, eggplant, peppers, and more.

- Leafy greens: spinach, kale, collards, arugula, swiss chard, and others.

✦ Organic, grass-fed, chemical-free, hormone-free, antibiotic-free and GMO-free beef, poultry, meat, and dairy products.[7]

✦ Wild fish from pristine waters, or organic-fed, hormone-free, antibiotic-free, GMO-free farm-raised fish.

✦ Cold-pressed, GMO-free vegetable oils such as olive or flax oils.

SEA VEGETABLES (FROM CLEAN, PRISTINE WATERS):

Sea vegetables such as kelp, nori, and seaweed (most often found in Asian restaurants or foods) are an excellent source of trace elements, vitamins, minerals and protein. However in light of industrial oil and chemical spills, the Fukishima radiation plume, and other sources of saltwater contamination, it is important to know the source of the sea vegetables.

7. If consuming animal protein, please be mindful that a diet that exceeds 5% in animal protein has been linked to cancer, even if the animal protein is organic and GMO-free. See page 30.

NATURAL SWEETENERS:

Honey, stevia, agave, maple syrup. Local raw honey has antibacterial properties and also alleviates allergies due to pollen. Stevia has a low glycemic index and is beneficial to those suffering from blood sugar imbalances. Agave has received mixed reviews due to its high glycemic index. Pure maple syrup is rich in essential vitamins and minerals.

NUTS, SEEDS AND WHOLE GRAINS:

These include almonds, walnuts, pistachios, pumpkin seeds, chia seeds, sunflower seeds, oats, barley, rice, and more. Almonds are now pasteurized in the United States, therefore much of their nutritional value is lost. Raw almonds may be purchased in the United States from California growers, within the state of California, or imported from Spain. Look for raw unsalted nuts and seeds. Many restaurants toast or bake nuts and seeds which destroy their nutritional value.

SUPERFOODS:

Superfood is the new buzzword in healthy eating. These foods or ingredients are nutritional powerhouses: extremely high in antioxidants, vitamins & minerals, and essential fatty acids. They can be hard to find on the road, especially in their raw optimum form. But I include it here in case you have access to a health food store in your travels, or choose to bring snacks with you. Superfoods include coconut, raw cacao (raw chocolate), chia seeds, goji berries, avocado, raw honey, sprouts, barley and wheat grass, leafy greens such as kale, spinach, collards and buckwheat.[8]

---

8. See David Wolfe, Superfoods, and http://www.superfoodsrx.com/superfoods/
   See http://www.livestrong.com/article/347949-what-are-dr-perricones-10-super-foods/

RAW OR SLOW-COOKED FOODS:

Cooking at high heat destroys the enzymes in foods and alters the nutrients in vegetables. This action decreases the bioavailability of nutrients. It also requires the body to work harder to digest the foods because the body now has to produce the needed enzymes for digestion (that were originally attached to the uncooked food). Raw foods are heated to less than 115F degrees to preserve the enzymes, while slow cooking preserves the nutrients of vegetables.

FERMENTED FOODS AND DRINKS:

These include sauerkraut (as long as it's not pasteurized), kombucha, kefir, kimchee, horseradish, pickles, and more. Fermented foods are generally an acquired taste. Some people love kimchee and others hate it. Your taste buds will tell you which fermented foods work for you! Also if you are a beer drinker, start asking for non-pasteurized beer. These are more readily available at microbreweries (although nouri at microbreweries may be hard to find), and some beers on tap like Samuel Adams are unpasteurized.

UNPROCESSED FOODS THAT HAVE NOT BEEN PASTEURIZED, IRRADIATED, OR ARTIFICIALLY PRESERVED:

These include raw milk and cheeses. Dairy products have developed a reputation of being unhealthy because they have been pasteurized. The pasteurization process destroys all the enzymes which when consumed by the body require the body to produce the lactase enzyme needed to digest the lactose in dairy products. In some instances people who think they are lactose intolerant are really allergic to the milk proteins that have changed in the pasteurization process.

Nouri Graph: Proportions for Eating Healthy

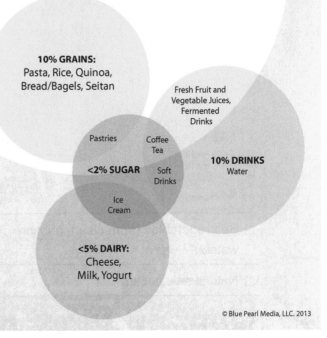

<5% MEATS:
Steak, Fish, Chicken, Pork, Turkey, Ham

<1% FRIED FOOD
Fried Meat
Fried Tofu
French Fries

<1% TOFU/SOY

80% PLANTS:
Almonds, Walnuts, Sunflower Seeds, Pumpkin Seeds, Chia Seeds, Flax Seeds, Kale, Chard, Collards, Spinach, Squash, Tomatoes, Potatoes, Eggplant, Carrots, Broccoli, Beans, Cauliflower, Parsnip, Corn, Herbs, Berries, Melons, Citrus, Apples, Peaches, Plums, Dates, Fig, Banana, Coconut, Avocado

10% GRAINS:
Pasta, Rice, Quinoa, Bread/Bagels, Seitan

Fresh Fruit and Vegetable Juices, Fermented Drinks

Pastries
Coffee Tea

<2% SUGAR
Soft Drinks

10% DRINKS
Water

Ice Cream

<5% DAIRY:
Cheese, Milk, Yogurt

A nouri meal does not require you to have each food category represented at all times. However, a nouri-based diet does require that 80% of your daily diet is made up of fresh fruits and vegetables, whole nuts, seeds and grains. That leaves 20% to allocate across meats, dairy, drinks and sugar.

If you are going to eat fried foods (not recommended) make sure that it is less than 1% of your daily intake.

By definition nouri means non-GMO, non chemically treated, whole foods.

Figure 3

TABLE **3**

Are You Eating Nouri? Does your diet primarily consist of:

FOOD CATEGORY	AS IT MAY APPEAR ON A MENU
☐ Organic and GMO-free foods	☐ Organic* fruits, organic greens, organic ingredients, organically sourced. Organic, pasture-raised chicken, grass-fed beef, wild game, wild salmon. ☐ Look for the following logos on food products and on restaurant menus: Check http://www.nongmoproject.org/find-non-gmo/find-restaurants/ for Non-GMO verified restaurants. At the time of publication the selection was limited to Berkeley, California and Seattle, Washington as they continue to build their database. Certified Naturally Grown certification is a grass roots alternative to Certified Organic, for farmers that grow organically but cannot afford the organic certification. *Natural is NOT the same as Organic.
☐ Sea vegetables (from clean, pristine waters)	☐ Seaweed salad, sushi rolls (nori-seaweed paper), hijiki salad
☐ Natural sweeteners	☐ Agave, maple syrup, honey, stevia

FOOD CATEGORY	AS IT MAY APPEAR ON A MENU
☐ Nuts, seeds, and whole grains	☐ Toasted almonds, candied walnuts, oatmeal, hot buckwheat cereal, granola, pumpkin seeds, toasted pepitas, sunflower seeds, almond milk, barley stew, quinoa, wild rice.
☐ Superfoods	☐ Guacamole, green smoothie, non-alcoholic pina colada, alfalfa sprouts on sandwich or salad, spinach or kale salad, side of swiss chard, chia pudding, coconut curry.
☐ Raw or slow-cooked foods	☐ Indian menu: korma, masala, saag, tandoori; Fruit salad, garden salad, mixed salad; Raw desserts: sorbet, gelato (real gelato is made with natural fruit sugars), almond milk.
☐ Fermented foods and drinks	☐ Kombucha, kefir, unpasteurized beer, sauerkraut, kimchee.
☐ Unprocessed foods that have not been pasteurized, irradiated, or artificially preserved.	☐ Raw milk cheese. Fresh, local, organic farm to table fruits and vegetables.

TABLE 4

Nouri Impact on the Body: Is It Worth the Benefit?

	IMPROVES CELLULAR FUNCTION/ REJUVENATES CELLS	MAINTAINS OR IMPROVES METABOLIC FUNCTION	MAINTAINS OPTIMUM WEIGHT	INCREASES ENERGY
Fresh, chemical-free whole fruits and vegetables (organic)	✓	✓	✓	✓
Organic and GMO-free foods		✓		
Sea vegetables (from clean, pristine waters)	✓	✓		
Sweeteners: Honey, Stevia, Agave, Maple Syrup*		✓		
Nuts, seeds, and whole grains**	✓	✓		
Superfoods	✓	✓	✓	✓
Raw or slow-cooked foods	✓	✓		✓
Fermented foods and drinks***	✓	✓	✓	✓
Unprocessed foods (have not been pasteurized, irradiated, or artificially preserved)		✓		

*Any excess consumption of natural sweeteners, with the exception of Stevia, can lead to blood sugar imbalances.

**Raw, soaked nuts and seeds are the easiest for the body to digest, and result in the greatest bioavailability of nutrients.

***Kombucha has been shown to return the body to homeostasis including optimum weight.

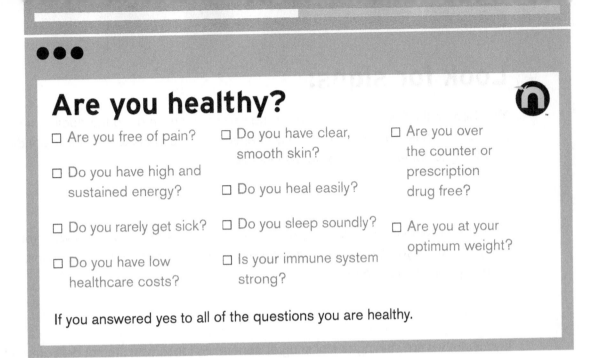

Are you healthy?

- ☐ Are you free of pain?
- ☐ Do you have high and sustained energy?
- ☐ Do you rarely get sick?
- ☐ Do you have low healthcare costs?
- ☐ Do you have clear, smooth skin?
- ☐ Do you heal easily?
- ☐ Do you sleep soundly?
- ☐ Is your immune system strong?
- ☐ Are you over the counter or prescription drug free?
- ☐ Are you at your optimum weight?

If you answered yes to all of the questions you are healthy.

Figure 4

What is Your Body or Mind Telling You?

Many of us receive little mind messages that say, "I'm in the mood for french fries," or "I'm craving pizza," or "I want a big juicy steak," even though we know it is not the healthiest option. A quick "is it worth the damage" calculation will cause you to pause and make a wise choice in that moment. See Quick Food Choice Calculator on page 51. But more importantly, what is your body telling you when you eat unhealthy versus nouri? Are you even listening? While the mind says one thing, the body may react differently. For example your body will either feel energized or lethargic. If you suffer from allergies, unhealthy foods may exacerbate the condition, while nouri may relieve it. This is a radical concept for many people, especially when new to the concept of eating nouri–and food as medicine.

Look for signs:

Your body will tell you something is wrong before you even go to the doctor, or sign up for invasive tests. You just need to pay attention. Visible signs to look for that indicate your body is not functioning properly include:

SKIN:

Your skin is your largest organ. If your liver and kidneys are not working well, you will see it in your skin. If you are developing patches, rashes, dry skin, or skin eruptions, there is probably something wrong.

WEIGHT:

If your clothes are starting to feel snug or abnormally loose (you are not deliberately trying to gain or lose weight), there is probably something wrong. Don't just go out and buy bigger or smaller sized clothes, or think it is ok to swim in or to burst out of the seams of your current wardrobe. In particular, if your waist exceeds 46 inches for a man or 42 inches for a woman, you are already in trouble. At this waist size your internal organs are compromised and not able to function properly, which is the beginning of illness and disease.

ALLERGIES:

Are you experiencing more allergies than normal, or developing allergic reactions to foods you have been eating for years? More and more people are experiencing strange illnesses that doctors cannot pinpoint. Much of these new illnesses are directly tied to the foods we eat.

THE COLOR OF YOUR TONGUE:

A healthy human tongue is pinkish in color and is gently moist with a light coating. A tongue that is unusual in color may be an indication of some problem in the body. Lack of water, vitamins, stress, and fatigue, can also lead to slight color changes of the tongue.

What is Your Healthy Eating KPI?

There are different ways to measure health. The traditional medical key performance indicators (KPIs)—for example blood pressure, cholesterol level, and triglyceride levels—help in determining acute conditions. These KPIs measure symptoms. Many people ask, "how do you measure the impact of food?" There are many tests performed by nutritionally enlightened practitioners that can achieve this. However, there is a better, cheaper, non-invasive way of measuring your overall health and the impact of your food choices that does not require a doctor's office, clinic or lab. It is called an Antioxidant Score. That is my health barometer.

A high antioxidant score is indicative of a strong immune system. Antioxidants latch onto damaged cells (free radicals) and act as a defense against slow poisons from poor food choices and environmental toxins. Antioxidants are found in fresh fruits, vegetables, leafy greens, and green and white tea.

The average antioxidant score is 24,000. Mine is 81,000, which is the result of a nouri lifestyle – a diet of fresh fruits and vegetables, juicing once to twice a day, and eating superfoods such as chia seeds and goji berries. I now rarely take a multivitamin (but did so for many years). I take extra Vitamin C and some other supplements when I feel overly stressed or when I am traveling a lot. What I particularly like about this barometer is that it adjusts for external circumstances outside of diet that affect the body's immune system. I have watched this number fluctuate over the years and the fluctuations are correlated with what's going on in my life—high stress, a lot of travel, skipping my regular juicing, getting off my yoga schedule, etc.

I am interested in the strength of my immune system. If you feed your immune system, everything else will come into balance.

I was first exposed to the Biophotonic Antioxidant Scanner in 2004. Pharmanex, a nutritional supplement division of Nuskin, had just commercialized the scanner. The technology was developed by the University of Utah for the purpose of determining macular degeneration of the eyes. My friend was a distributor for Pharmanex and was insistent for a long time that I try out the scanner. He claimed that "based on your lifestyle and eating habits, I bet you will score pretty high." I finally succumbed, and said to myself, "well if I score high then it validates my lifestyle, and if I score low the problem is their technology." As it turned out, I scored 54,000. I outscored everyone in the state of Colorado at the time. Vegans typically score the highest in the 90,000 range. My lowest score was 48,000 in 2008, which was a particularly difficult time in my life.

On average a scan will cost you between $5-10.[9] Depending on your baseline health you may need to monitor your blood sugar, blood pressure, or triglyceride levels. If you have not been to a doctor recently, and your antioxidant score is particularly low, in the 10,000 range or lower, it could be indicative of a serious medical issue.

9. You can find a biophotonic scanner near you at: http://www.nuskin.com/en_US/products/pharmanex/scanner.html

Healthy Eating Spectrum

 NEGATIVE IMPACT ←————————————→ POSITIVE IMPACT

Foods

| | FACTORY FARM MEAT & POULTRY | | ORGANIC GRASS-FED MEAT, POULTRY | |
| GMO & CHEMICALLY TREATED FOOD | *Hormones & Antibiotics* | FARM-RAISED FISH & SHRIMP | & DAIRY | WHOLE FRUITS & VEGETABLES |

←—————————————————————————————————

| FAST FOOD | PROCESSED PACKAGED FOOD | PASTRIES & SWEETS | WILD-CAUGHT FISH & SHRIMP (FROM CLEAN WATERS) | ORGANIC NON-GMO FOODS | SUPER FOODS |
| | *Potato Chips, Processed Lunch Meats* | *Ice Cream* | | | |

Beverages

| ENERGY DRINKS & SHAKES | | | ORGANIC FRESH FRUIT & | |
| *Caffeine & Sugar Based* | JUICE DRINKS *Sugar Sweetened* | SMOOTHIES | VEGETABLE JUICE | WATER |

←—————————————————————————————————

| SODA, DIET SODA | ALCOHOL | COFFEE | TEA *Green, White, Herbal Infusions* | FERMENTED DRINKS |

Preparation

| | USE OF HFCS, MSG, SALT, GMO | SLOW | |
| FRIED WITH BAD OILS | INGREDIENTS | COOKED | FERMENTED |

←—————————————————————————————————

| DEEP FRIED | COOKED AT HIGH TEMPERATURE *Stir Fry* | BAKED | STEAMED | RAW *Not Heated Above 115°, Unpasteurized* |

© Blue Pearl Media, LLC. 2013

Figure 5

49

QUICK FOOD CHOICE CALCULATOR

Pilots have to make a number of decisions/calculations very quickly regarding wind speed, air speed, air pressure, etc. They are constantly monitoring variables to ensure a safe flight. That same kind of quick calculation is needed when looking at a menu. It is very easy to be overwhelmed by seemingly delicious menu choices. However, being able to scan a menu quickly, and rapidly calculate the following 7 variables will make your food choices infinitely easier.

1. **INGREDIENTS:** GMO? Oils used? Fresh or canned? Organic?

2. **NUTRIENT VALUE:** whole food or processed?

3. **HOW THE FOOD IS PREPARED:** deep fried, steamed, baked, broiled, boiled, raw, slow-cooked, stir-fried?

4. **IMPACT ON THE BODY:** Positive (low impact), Negative (high impact), Neutral?

5. **CONTEXT:** What did I have earlier, yesterday, during the week?

6. **DETOX:** Can I compensate later for any damage now? Yes/No

7. **CHOICE:** Is it worth the damage? Yes/No

Ultimately you are looking to make a thumbs up or thumbs down decision. See Table 5 Menu Scan and Food Choice Calculator Example for how you can put this quick calculator into effect at a restaurant.

TABLE **5**

Menu scan and food choice calculator example: Chips, salsa and guacamole

VARIABLE	QUICK CALCULATION	ANSWER
Ingredients: GMO? Oils used? Fresh or canned? Organic?	The chips are probably made from GMO corn, the guacamole is either fresh (better flavor and more nutritional) or pre-made or packaged. The salsa is most likely from a bottle and not freshly made.	Avocados: Fresh Corn tortilla chips: Likely GMO Salsa: canned tomatoes
Nutrient Value: Whole food or processed?	Tortilla chips have little nutritional value, probably made from GMO corn, and high in salt. The freshly made guacamole is a whole food (if it was prepackaged not sure what else is in it). The salsa is made from whole foods, but the tomatoes are likely to be canned, with a little less taste and nutritional value.	Fresh avocado: High Corn tortilla chips: Low Salsa: Medium
How the Food is Prepared: Deep fried, steamed, baked, broiled, boiled, raw, slow-cooked, stir-fried?	Tortilla chips were either baked or fried; avocado is uncooked; tomatoes were probably cooked.	Avocado and tomatoes outweigh the corn tortilla chips.

VARIABLE	QUICK CALCULATION	ANSWER
Impact on the Body: Positive (low impact), Negative (high impact), Neutral	Corn tortilla chips: negative Avocados: Positive Salsa: Neutral (if cooked and canned); Positive if freshly made	Compromise
Context: What did I have earlier, yesterday, during the week?	Pizza, salad, Thai, Indian	Go easy on the chips
Detox: Can I compensate later for any damage now? Yes/No	I will be home next week.	Yes.
Choice: Is it worth the damage? Yes/No	Avocados are a superfood and fresh made guacamole is delicious and worth the corn chip damage today.	Yes. Go easy on the chips, but overall good choice.

TRAVEL TIPS

Eating healthy on the road requires you to commit to three planning and critical thinking steps, and three action steps. The Eat Healthy Travel Wheel illustrates these six steps.

These six steps are actually 5 tips on how to become a nouri seeker on the road. The last tip on detox is a bit of an insurance policy if you will. More on that later. Each tip comes with suggestions on how to put them into action.

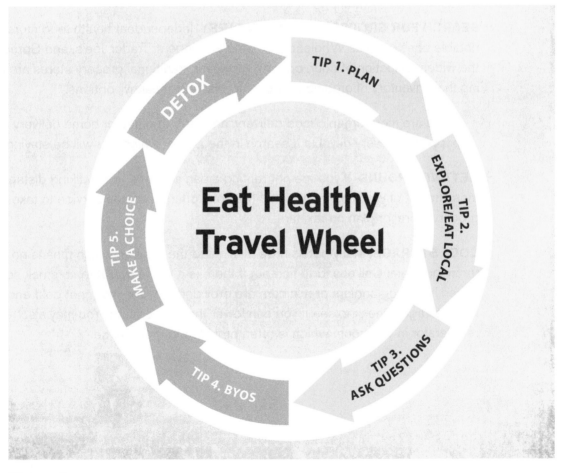

Figure 6

TIP 1. PLAN AHEAD

→ **WHEN POSSIBLE AVOID THE CORPORATE HOTEL.** While some corporate hotels are getting better on the healthy food front, it is always better to retain as much control as you can over what you eat. Find an apartment or bed and breakfast where you can prepare your own meals as if you were home.

- Search for Corporate Housing by Owner (http://www.corporatehousingbyowner.com/) or Vacation Rental by Owner (www.vrbo.com)

→ **SEARCH FOR GROCERY STORES NEARBY.** Independent health food stores and notable ones such as WholeFoods, Natural Grocers, Trader Joe's, and Sprouts, offer the widest selection of nouri options. However, traditional grocery stores are increasing their inventory of organic produce, foods, and "healthy" options.

- There are more organic food delivery, and farm to office or home delivery services popping up every day. Do a search in the area in which you will be staying.

→ **GETTING AROUND.** If you are not renting a car, and little is in walking distance or mass transit of your hotel: find out if the hotel offers a shuttle service to take you to the grocery store, or plan on taxi fare.

→ **COOL STORAGE.** Many hotels have eliminated the minibar, which means no refrigerator in the room. Call ahead to find out if there is a fridge available, to stock some food. When beverage coolers or minibars are provided they are often not cold enough for food storage. Check to see if you can lower the temperature. You may also request a refrigerator in your room which is often provided free of charge.

TIP 2. EXPLORE AND EAT LOCAL

➔ **LOOK FOR HEALTHY RESTAURANTS:** According to the National Restaurant Association's *What's Hot in 2012 Survey*, four of the top five trends were locally sourced meats and seafood, locally grown produce, hyper-local sourcing, and sustainability. Despite these encouraging trends, finding a healthy restaurant is still a challenge because healthy dining falls into so many different categories. However, online sources such as Yelp and Urban Spoon are getting better. Some search terms for the Internet, Mobile apps, or online restaurant guides include: farm-to-table, locavore restaurants, health conscious restaurants, seasonal menu, organic ingredients, raw foods, vegetarian and vegan (although vegetarian does not imply healthy, but you should be able to find some hearty salads and soups). If you find yourself in what appears to be a challenging area, ask the locals for where the hippies live and eat. That should point you in the right direction.

- **TRUE FOOD KITCHEN** is a restaurant concept developed by Dr. Andrew Weil and restauranteur Sam Fox that focuses on an anti-inflammatory Mediterranean diet. Currently True Food Kitchen restaurants are in California, Arizona and Colorado. Check out their website for locations http://www.foxrc.com/restaurants/true-food-kitchen/

- **TOP 10 FARM-TO-TABLE RESTAURANTS** in the United States according to Epicurious http://www.epicurious.com/articlesguides/diningtravel/restaurants/farmtotable_intro

- **THE AMERICAN FARM-TO-TABLE RESTAURANT GUIDE** is an online restaurant guide of restaurants that source ingredients locally as much as possible. It is not exhaustive, but it is a very good start for a number of cities. http://www.american-farmtotable.com/

- **HEALTHYDININGFINDER.COM** is a website dedicated to identifying healthier options at primarily restaurant chains. It is a good start, although its definition of healthy is not as specific as ours. In particular, it does not take into consideration how the ingredients were grown and produced (e.g whether non-GMO or organic).

- **SPECIALTY FOOD TRUCKS** are on the rise all over North America. Many newly launched trucks are focused on providing healthy, organic options. There are several mobile apps now available that allow you to track down food trucks. This may be an option for a quick meal in between appointments.

  » *TruxMap tracks food trucks in 34 U.S. and 2 Canadian cities, using tweets to show where food trucks are located as well as where they are going. The maps show where food trucks are open and where food trucks will open shortly. Available for iPhone, iPad, and Android. In addition, there is a mobile web application for some cities for those on other mobile devices.*

  » *Eat St. mobile app builds on the Food Networks Eat St. TV series. It claims to have the largest food truck database in North America. The reviews of the app are mixed, but it is a good way to discover new trucks. Available for iPhone only, or use the mobile web app.*

  » *Street Food drills down to the details of each city's local food truck scene, showing food trucks on a real-time map, including their opening hours (so you know how long they will be there!). Individual mobile apps for Boston, Calgary, Toronto, and Vancouver available. User ratings are consistently positive for all four cities. Available for iPhone and iPad.*

- **LOOK FOR ETHNIC RESTAURANTS.** Ethnic foods that are primarily vegetable based are: Mexican, Indian, Asian (Vietnamese,Thai, Chinese, Malaysian, Indonesian), Mediterranean/Greek, Middle Eastern/Moroccan/N. African.

- **LOOK FOR RESTAURANT DELIVERY SERVICES.** Look for restaurants near you that will deliver. There are three good websites and mobile apps in the US that will locate restaurants near you (by your specific address) that deliver, allow you to search by cuisine, and place an order directly from the menu. Eat24 is the only one that provides delivery from organic restaurants in 12 states and 20 cities.

  » https://delivery.com – *Android and iPhone app available*

  » http://eat24hours.com/organic – *iPhone, Android, Kindle, iPad app available*

  » https://Grubhub.com – *iPhone and Android app available*

✈ **EAT LOCAL:** Take advantage of traveling to different places and cultures. Generally, eating local means that you have access to the freshest food. If an area is known for seafood or wild game go for that. Avoid eating seafood in areas that primarily produce and consume meat, unless there is known high turnover for seafood. And vice-versa for areas that are known for seafood rather than meat.

Now, depending on where your travels take you this could be a good or bad idea due to local cooking customs, local bacteria and parasites, environmental incidents–think BP oil spill, and Fukishima nuclear radiation disaster in Japan. Be aware of local culinary style. Just because deep fried chicken is a local favorite, doesn't mean that it is healthy!

TIP 3. ASK QUESTIONS

→ **WHAT'S IT WORTH?** Why are you eating–for health or just to eat? There are direct and indirect costs associated with our food choices. Is the sandwich worth $10–net present value and future value in terms of the impact it will have on you? Research has shown that every $1 spent on unhealthy food results in $5 of healthcare costs in the future. What is it worth to you now and tomorrow?

Every time you make a food purchase you should think in terms of value, which is very closely tied to the notion of "is it worth the damage". Whether your food choice at that particular moment is fatty, processed, GMO-based, full of hormones or pesticides, high in sugar or salt, there is a short-term and long term cost associated with it. I know there are times that I will opt to eat something that I haven't had in a really long time, and I say to myself, "I'm going to regret this later." That regret can be in the form of some late night gastro-distress, bloating and inflammation, or collective damage that won't manifest for some time. See Table 2 Unhealthy Food Impact on the Body: Is It Worth the Damage?

→ **DON'T BE AFRAID TO ASK YOUR WAITPERSON, THE MANAGER OR CHEF QUESTIONS.** Most people with food allergies or who follow strict diets due to various ailments such as celiac, diabetes, cardiovascular, or other diseases are not shy about asking for modifications to dishes or about specific ingredients. As one family restaurant owner said to me, "it's not like it used to be. Customers should feel free to ask questions and seek modifications". Without questions and concerns restaurants cannot improve. So don't be shy. However, if you get an answer that you do not like, and you don't feel the meal is worth the damage – you must be willing to order something else, and if the restaurant cannot accommodate you, to leave.

Restaurant Checklist

This can be uncomfortable for many people, but if you really want to know what you are eating at a restaurant, ask your waitperson these general questions:

☐ Are your ingredients organic?

☐ Are your ingredients non-GMO?

☐ What oils do you use?

☐ What processed food ingredients do you use?

☐ Do you use MSG?

☐ Do you source directly from local farms or go through a wholesale distributor?

Figure 7

TIP 4. BRING YOUR OWN SNACKS

This sounds like such a new age, hippie thing to do, but it really works. If you make health bars at home, bring those with you. Otherwise buy a case of your favorite health bars (remember to make sure they are whole fruit and nut bars sweetened with honey, agave, or stevia).

TIP 5. MAKE A CHOICE

→ **CHANGE YOUR PERSPECTIVE.** Focus on the nutrients in the food. With this perspective, your expectations of what consists of a meal, what is satisfying, and what constitutes value for portion size will change. You can always find something in the bleakest of circumstances that won't cause too much damage. The body is resilient, and will heal itself, but you need to give it the opportunity to do so.

→ **AT THE AIRPORT, TRAIN OR FERRY STATION.** Airport food is the biggest challenge. Not only is it mostly processed food that is available – it is also x-rayed, which reduces any nutrient value of the food. Look for fruits, salads, nuts, low impact sandwiches (remember that unless otherwise stated, anything with meats and cheeses are probably the product of factory-farm animals, which means the sandwich is full of antibiotics, chemicals, and/or GMOs). Look for juice bars. Don't settle for the first place you see once you've passed security. If you have time, explore the terminal; it's also an opportunity for a little exercise.

→ **MINIMIZE THE MEALS YOU HAVE TO EAT OUT.** If you are fortunate enough to stay in a condo or hotel with a kitchenette and have the time, try to prepare your own meals as much as you can. If you have not indulged or overtaxed your body on this trip then feel free to dine worry-free. If you want or need to be extra diligent, then try to eat something nouri before you head out to your lunch or dinner commitments to avoid the temptations of the menu.

→ **BE WILLING TO PAY MORE.** While organic foods are now competitively priced against conventional foods (at least at the grower level), it is still a small portion of the market (less than 15%). Therefore, you should still expect to pay more at grocery stores, and restaurants that source from organic suppliers, or promote farm to table practices.

TIP 6. DETOX

There is really no way to be healthy on the road without instituting some sort of detox program either on the road or when you get home. Compensating for damage done by food choices today involves eliminating toxins and metabolic wastes from the body. Here are some detox options for you to consider. Find out what works best for you:

→ **DRINK LOTS OF QUALITY WATER.** Water is your greatest detoxifier and ensures that your cells function properly. Opt for water instead of soft drinks or sugared juices. If you don't like the taste of water at first, try adding lemon or lime to it. If you have other fruits available such as strawberries or melons, for instance from a fruit cup, drop it into your water.

→ **FAST ONE DAY A WEEK.** Water fasts are very hard on the body. Instead, focus on a liquid fast that includes fresh juices and soups (avoid canned soups that are high in salt, MSG, and fats). A one-day fast is easy, and even welcomed when there are not a lot of healthy food options available. However, fasting any more than one day usually requires the appropriate mental state. Be mindful that stress, along with a disrupted routine can stimulate hunger.

→ **EAT A RAW FOOD DIET FOR ONE WEEK WHEN YOU GET HOME.** If you can do it on the road, all the better.

→ **CLEAN OUT YOUR INTESTINAL TRACT AND COLON,** especially after a trip where you feel like you ate difficult to digest foods.

- **SALT WASH:** This will purge your entire intestinal tract, including all the nasties that hide in the nooks and crannies of the intestinal wall. Be sure to replenish your intestinal flora afterwards with probiotics such as acidophilous, kombucha, or kefir. Add 1 tablespoon of celtic sea salt to one quart of warm water. This is like drinking seawater, but yes drink it all. Wait about 30 minutes, and you should feel the need to evacuate quickly. If no movement in 30 minutes drink another cup of water and move around a bit to activate the bowels.

- **ENEMA OR COLONIC:** This is an uncomfortable topic for many people. But if you want to be clean from the inside out and eliminate toxic build up in your gut, you need to get comfortable with this. Colonics and enemas are therapies that both involve introducing water into the colon through the rectum in order to cleanse the colon; but they are different. Enemas can be self-administered, while colonics must be administered by a trained colon hydrotherapist. Do some research to see what might work best for you.

→ **DRINK PROBIOTIC DRINKS SUCH AS KOMBUCHA OR KEFIR.** Probiotics are millions to billions of good bacteria that work to detox the body and bring it back into balance. You can also eat fermented foods such as sauerkraut, which are a great source of probiotics. Make sure the sauerkraut is unpasteurized. If it is pasteurized then you will not be *RECEIVING ANY OF ITS BENEFITS.* Fermented drinks and foods are an acquired taste, so experiment. Start asking restaurants if they carry kombucha or kefir drinks.

→ **DRINK CHIA SEEDS IN WATER WITH LEMON AND HONEY OR AGAVE.** Not only are chia seeds a great detoxifier, but this drink is the energy drink of the famous Tarahumara runners. You can also sprinkle them on salads. Chia seeds are a great superfood to bring with you on a trip. For the drink: squeeze 1/2 of a lemon or lime into 8 ounces of water, add 1 teaspoon of chia seeds and 1 tablespoon of honey or 1 teaspoon of agave, and stir. Tastes better chilled or over ice.

→ **DRINK GREEN TEA OR WHITE TEA** which is loaded with polyphenol antioxidants that scavenge for free radicals.

→ **DRINK HOT WATER WITH LEMON** every morning and every evening. This is a great detoxifier and aids with digestion after a heavy meal.

→ **CLEANSE YOUR LIVER** by taking milk thistle, dandelion, or burdock in the form of supplements, tea, or tincture.

→ **CLEANSE YOUR BLOOD** by taking red clover in the form of supplements, tea, or tincture.

TABLE 6

Nouri Alternatives Guide

This guide was inspired from the Healthy Alternatives Guide developed by James Colquhoun and Laurentine ten Bosch of Food Matters.

THE USUAL	OPTIONS WHEN AT HOME OR WHEN LODGING INCLUDES A KITCHENETTE	OPTIONS ON THE ROAD
Cows milk and cheese	Almond milk, hemp milk, brazil nut milk, oat milk, nut cheese, raw (unpasteurized) organic milk and cheeses (cow, goat, sheep), organic yogurt	Almond milk, organic milk and cheeses, goat cheese, organic yogurt If none available, ask is it worth the damage?
Cereal	Whole oats, granola, muesli, buckwheat	Sugar-free granola, and oatmeal
Sandwich with mayonnaise, butter	Hummus, guacamole, pesto	
Pasta Bowl	Spelt, quinoa or buckwheat pasta, rice noodles, spiralized raw zucchini squash	Wild rice bowl, veggie bowl. Limit pasta intake and ask is it worth the damage?
White Rice	Organic brown rice*, wild rice or quinoa	
Steak	Wild fish, portobella mushrooms, local wild game, grass-fed beef	
Chicken	Organic pasture-raised chicken	
White Sugar	Stevia, agave, raw honey	Stevia, agave, honey

*With run off from pesticides, studies have shown that rice absorbs more arsenic than other vegetables. Limit intake if it is not grown organically.

THE USUAL	OPTIONS WHEN AT HOME OR WHEN LODGING INCLUDES A KITCHENETTE	OPTIONS ON THE ROAD
Table salt	Sea salt, organic tamari or soy sauce	Avoid additional salt
Coffee and Tea	Chicory, organic decaf coffee, white or green tea, herbal tea, red tea, herbal chai, organic coffee, yerba mate	Green, white or red (roobois) tea, yerba maté, decaf coffee, herbal chai (see milk and sweetener alternatives above)
Soft drinks	Herbal iced tea, water, fresh fruit and vegetable juices, probiotic drinks	Water, fresh squeezed juice, probiotic drink, sparkling water with lemon or lime
Milk shakes	Smoothie (non-dairy, unless organic—see milk alternatives above)	
Unhealthy snacks: chips, dips, biscuits, chocolate bars, etc.	Hummus & pita, olive tapenade, guacamole	Dried fruit & nut health bar, nuts, fruits, kale chips
Unhealthy desserts: ice cream, cakes, pastries	Coconut macaroons, non-dairy coconut ice cream, organic ice cream, raw desserts made from dates, nuts, and fresh fruits	Smoothie, raw desserts, gelato (real gelato is made from the natural sugars of whole fruits, not refined sugar). Always ask is it worth the damage?
Beer and alcohol	Limit intake, but look for unpasteurized beer in microbreweries or on tap. When ordering wine in restaurants, look for local wines as small local wineries do not pasteurize their wines. Wines below 14% alcohol content may be pasteurized.	

TRAVELING THROUGH NOURI DESERTS

AS A ROAD WARRIOR YOU INEVITABLY ENCOUNTER
THE FOLLOWING NOURI DESERTS:

→ **AIRPORTS.** Why can't airports negotiate healthy concessions? Some airports are doing better jobs than others. For example, the JetBlue terminal at JFK in New York, and Chicago O'Hare plans an overhaul of its food offerings to be healthier pursuant to a new report Putting Sustainability on the Table: AIRPORT WORKERS' VISION FOR $3 BILLION OF FOOD AND DRINK AT O'HARE.

→ **CONFERENCE CENTERS.** Conference food has to be one of the worst tasting food options on the road. There are some instances where they provide some semblance of good nutritious food. However, as conference organizers work to reduce costs in a difficult economic climate, the food seems to be getting worse or simply disappearing altogether. The box lunch is quickly becoming the norm—chips, nasty sandwich, and cookies.

→ **FOOD COURTS AND FAST FOOD CHAINS.** They generally serve high fat, high salt, high sugar foods.

→ **HOTEL ROOM SERVICE.** It generally offers a very limited menu.

→ **VENDING MACHINES.** They are essentially dispensaries for sugar, fat and salt.

→ **AIRPLANES.** Need I say more?

When I first got on my health kick, I started traveling with cases of Larabars. I soon started traveling with just a few bars. Now, I don't travel with them anymore, as I've been able to control my appetite and make informed choices based on the circumstances. Now that you can bring food on the plane, if I have the luxury of being able to prepare something at home, I do.

In Transit Tips

✈ Try to eat something before you leave the house. If you know you are going to be at the airport or on the plane around lunch time or dinner time; try to eat something before you get to the airport when you will have more choice.

✈ At the airport (applies at train or bus station), look for a salad place, juice bar, cold snacks. Get the perfect oatmeal at Starbucks (be picky. For example, I ask for honey instead of brown sugar). KIND is a health bar (made of nuts and dried fruit) now available in most airports. KIND was founded because the CEO was tired of not finding anything healthy to eat at the airport. KIND is just one example of health bars now available at airports. Notice that I did not recommend airport restaurants. It is rare that the road warrior has time for a sit down meal at the airport unless she has an unusually long layover or the flight is seriously delayed. If you have the time to eat at an airport restaurant then remember the Quick Food Choice Calculator.

✈ On the plane, don't eat the pretzels, and don't drink the soft-drinks. The juices are full of sugar, so stay away from those too. Drink water. Drinking water on the plane helps with jet lag and also helps with adjusting to the dryness of the plane and to a high-altitude destination. On long-haul trans-oceanic flights, your best bet is to ask for a vegetarian meal. It's still not great but better than the normal fare.

1. YOU WALK INTO A COFFEE SHOP, STARVING:

↗ Scan the counter for a fruit cup, oatmeal or nut bars (I stay away from energy bars and "health bars" because they usually have a lot of fillers that I can't pronounce, or have sugar, molasses, vegetable oils (that are generally GMO). Nut bars made from raw nuts and dried fruits are great.

↗ If a fruit cup, oatmeal, or nut bar is not available, I usually ask myself, "how hungry am I really?" and "Can I wait until my next opportunity to eat?" I usually convince myself that a hot tea will suffice.

↗ If I am ready to chew my arm off, then I look for the yummiest thing around that will do the least damage. This gets really subjective, depending on your current situation. For me, I might go for the croissant or bagel (not ideal, but better than the sugar pastries). This is all relative of course. If the choice is between a sugar filled baked muffin or scone, I'll choose the croissant or bagel.

→ That was the food part, now what about the drinks? I personally do not drink coffee. But if you are a coffee drinker, then you need to think about what goes into the coffee and pay attention to the milk and sugar. That also goes for other coffee or tea lattes. If you are a latte addict, I would think about insisting upon organic milk. Contrary to all the marketing buzz around fat-free milk, if you are going to drink cow's milk, whole milk is better than 2% or fat free. Whole milk is healthier because many of the vitamins in milk are fat soluble. Drinking fat free or 2% milk means that all you are drinking is liquid calories. Soymilk is not the healthier option you may think it is; soymilk is generally made from GMO soy. Almond milk is increasingly being offered at independent coffee and tea shops. Ask for substitutes to the norm. Even if they don't have substitutes, you can make a choice, and your question sends a signal. When more then 10 people ask the same question, food establishments take note. Be aware that chai and chai lattes sold in most coffee shops are boxed or pre-mixed chai, which is made with lots of sugar, to which milk is added on site.

2. **YOU ARRIVE AT THE AIRPORT, HUNGRY AND STRESSED –** or just criss-crossed the airport terminals to make your connecting flight. All that is available is traditional food court fare and the not so helpful airport staff person tells you there is no hot food on the other side of security:

→ Whatever is on the other side of security cannot be worse then those choices. Have faith, you will find water, fruit cups, wraps, or salads on the other side.

→ You can decide that it's worth the damage in this situation.

3. YOU GET TO YOUR HOTEL ROOM AND YOU ARE STARVING AND LOOK AT THE ROOM SERVICE MENU:

→ Room service food is generally terrible *and* you pay at least a 30% premium for it. If you get to your hotel room at a reasonable time and have time to walk around, find a restaurant with healthier options nearby, or look for a WholeFoods or health food store equivalent. If the hotel has a refrigerator, stock up on some fruit cups, kombucha if you like that, granola (read the labels, and avoid the ones made with sugar and canola oil), and whatever suits your now nouri-minded fancy.

→ If you don't have the time, or are too tired to go out, think Take Out! Do a search on one of the delivery food services that will deliver to your location. See page 59.

→ You get in late and there is really no other option but room service. Let's say you get to the hotel after 9pm. You are either exhausted, or there really is nothing open. Remember that you will more than likely be going to sleep soon, so first thing you should be thinking about is something light. Also once you start eating, it usually only takes about 20 minutes for your stomach to signal that it is full – no matter what you eat, as long as you eat slowly. I will usually opt for the fruit plate, a veggie plate, or mixed green salad with balsamic vinaigrette. Pasta, breads, animal protein will be hard for the body to process. Because you are already tired, a big meal will put you to sleep quickly, but that it not necessarily optimum. Sandwiches, anything that has a lot of cheese and sauces will probably have GMO ingredients unless stated to be organic. Deep fried foods like french fries will be difficult for the body to digest.

4. THE STEWARDESS COMES BY WITH PRETZELS, SNACKS AND THE DRINK CART:

✈ Pass on the snacks, and ask for water if you did not bring it on the plane with you. Drinking water on the plane helps with jet lag if you are traveling internationally, it also helps with adjusting to the dryness of the plane. If you are flying to high altitude destinations like Denver, Colorado this will also help with adjusting to altitude when you land.

✈ Many people like to have beer, wine, or a cocktail on the plane. Alcohol stresses the liver, so just make your choices wisely. In addition, at cruising altitude alcohol acts more quickly on the body.

✈ Try to stay away from the juices and soft drinks as they are full of sugar.

5. CONFERENCE FOOD LOOKS UNAPPETIZING:

✦ The conference environment is quite challenging. Depending on your role at the conference, and the lighting at the venue, your appetite may be going crazy. You may have skipped breakfast to get to the session on time. You may have been up late preparing your 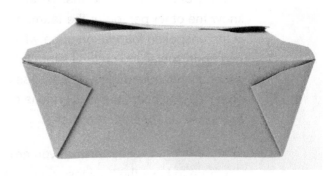 presentation or responding to emails. You are looking forward to a lunch break and unfortunately it is generally the dreaded box lunch or an unappetizing buffet. I almost always pass on the box lunch, which is invariably a sandwich, chips and a cookie. Sometimes you can luck out with a veggie wrap. When it comes to the buffet, I usually avoid things in sauces, and decide on what is going to be the bulk of my dish. In my case it is usually a salad or vegetables, and I work around that. If the soup is good, I'll have that. Stay away from lunch meats. If there is a lunch meat plate, I may take a slice of cheese along with some fruit and bread. When wraps are served, I go for the veggie wrap; again stay away from wraps with lunch meats. The combination of bread, salad, and vegetables usually has a filling effect. Walk away from the dessert table.

✦ Skip the conference lunch if the food is really bad. If short on time, go to the Starbucks in the hotel and get a bowl of oatmeal, or if you have time find a restaurant close by that serves healthier, if not tastier fare. If I planned ahead, I would head up to my hotel room and grab one of my snacks. Stashing a few health food bars in your briefcase is another way to make it through lunch, and look forward to a good dinner.

6. **BUSINESS DINNERS AND COCKTAILS.** Socializing after hours is often where the majority of business relationships are formed and nurtured. It is the ritual of getting to know the other person or the team, building trust, and respect. The business dinner is the unspoken foundation upon which professional relationships are built, which is tied up in social and cultural expectations. It is not about the food. It is about pride, impressions, boundaries, and assessment criteria in many parts of the world. When committed to nouri, the challenge is often how to avoid insulting hosts, or appearing anti-social. Here are a few tricks:

→ **Selecting a restaurant.** If you are fortunate enough to influence the decision on where to have the business dinner, select a restaurant that provides options for all.

→ **Drinks.** Unfortunately, there is still a great deal of peer pressure to drink alcohol in after-hours socializing. There are a few ways around this:

» *Order a drink, which satisfies your "social obligation" and don't touch it. No one will notice or care.*

» *Order non-pasteurized beer. As mentioned earlier, non-pasteurized beer is nouri in moderation. See Table 6 Nouri Alternatives Guide.*

» *Explain that you do not drink for religious or health reasons.*

→ **Appetizers.** Support the majority's choice in appetizers and order something that you want. No one will notice that you are not eating the other appetizers as they devour the plates. However, international travel can be more difficult where pride in local cuisine is a big factor. In this case, be open to trying anything, but explain up front that due to health reasons you limit your diet to for example vegetarian dishes. Women seem to have an easier time then men at setting these boundaries and having them respected (without having a negative effect on the business relationship). I have found in all my travels, that what is most important is showing your hosts respect.

USING CORPORATE INFLUENCE FOR SOLUTIONS

✈ According to the Global Business Traveler Association (GBTA) there were 454 million US business trips in 2012. Total US business travel spend is approximately $268.5 billion. That is just for the United States.[10] Road warriors and those responsible for managing business travel spend have enormous purchasing power. You can make a difference.

✈ Your lifestyle is being disrupted/uprooted by business travel. You have an expense account or per diem allocations when you travel; you might as well use it to your advantage. The average U.S. per diem for food is $85 per day and $142 per day outside of the United States.[11] Instead of wasting it on bad room service or traditional steakhouses and restaurants, find healthier options. Seek out the ethnic cuisines like Thai, Indian, Mediterranean, and farm-to-table restaurants that offer something for everyone. Find the local grocery store or health food store – seek out the nouri options.

✈ If you work for a large company, start exercising some corporate muscle and get whomever is responsible for travel budgets to request that preferred airlines and hotels offer organic, non-GMO, menu options. It all starts with a few voices.

✈ Airports are increasingly dependent on concession revenues. Change your focus to nouri and that will change what becomes available at airports.

✈ To the extent possible, direct travel to cities that support a nouri lifestyle and therefore provide more choice.

10. GBTA Foundation, GBTA-BTI™ Outlook–United States: Prospects for Domestic and International Outbound Business Travel 2013-2014 (2013 Q3)

11. Business Travel News, 2013 Corporate Travel Index, March 18, 2013.

✈ If you are responsible for corporate sponsorships at events and conferences that involve a breakfast, lunch or networking event, you have the power to influence the foods offered. A great place to start is by requiring that all the food be organic and non-GMO.

✈ Bring this book to the attention of your HR department and request that they purchase bulk copies to distribute to employees—especially the Sales, Business Development, Field operations, and Executive teams—to those departments that invariably have high travel budgets. Your health is important to the company from a productivity, morale, and healthcare cost perspective.

A commitment to eating healthy can frankly be overwhelming if you let it. There is a lot to think about, and you are not going to get it all right as long as you live in the modern world. You will make compromises almost everyday unless you can control your food supply—not just what you buy at the grocery store, but how it is grown and produced. The more you know, the more responsible you can be. The more responsible you are, the healthier you will be... and one person at a time we may even be able to redirect how food is grown and produced to ensure that it is in fact food... oops I meant nouri— nutrients that enable our cells to thrive instead of shrivel under a slow poisoning.

On the road and off the road... think nouri, not food!

Tips for relaxing, movement, energy and de-stressing while traveling

HOTEL ROOM WORKOUT:

Checkout this Lifehacker.com site for a simple workout you can do in your hotel room. There are 12 exercises to the routine, and a timed app was created to keep you on track and focused. http://lifehacker.com/these-12-videos-show-the-proper-form-for-a-7-minute-ful-499199366

YOGA FOR TRAVEL:

→ **IN THE PLANE, TRAIN OR BUS:** The seats in all of these situations, even first class, are less than comfortable. Airplane yoga can help. The Zen Guy has come to the rescue with Airplane Yoga, available in several formats (Amazon Kindle, Apple iBook, Nook, and iPhone app). There is also an Airplane yoga audio that comes in three versions: ten minutes, twenty minutes and thirty minutes available at: http://www.iamplify.com/store/bio/Amy-Ippoliti/products/author_id/106

What I have found most valuable is knowing and understanding some of these poses so that you can practice them when appropriate. For some people following the full routine works, for others, like me, I pick and choose depending on what is going on with my neck, shoulders, or back.

✈ WHEN YOU GET TO YOUR HOTEL ROOM:

1. The easiest and most effective restorative yoga pose I have found is legs up the wall.

- With a folded blanket, towel or pillow (support) start 5-6 inches from the wall. Sit sideways on the floor on one end of your support.

- Swing your legs up the wall as your shoulders and head come to rest on the ground. Your butt should be against the wall, and your sitting bones should be in the space between the support and the wall. The purpose of the blanket, towel or pillow support is for your thigh bones to drop down into your hip sockets. This pose is not about reversing your blood circulation because your feet are up in the air. This pose is about releasing tension in the body.

- If you need to adjust the support, place the feet on the wall with bent knees. Press into the wall as you lift the hips up and move the support as needed.

- Keep the legs vertical and allow your arms to rest naturally at your sides or shoulder height. Now here is the trick. Your feet should be active. Don't just hangout with floppy relaxed legs leaning against the wall. Flex your feet, feel your inner thighs tightened, and make sure your feet are parallel to each other. Your feet will now be slightly away from the wall.

- Stay in the pose for 5-15 minutes.

- To come out of the pose, slide your legs down the wall and roll over to your right side. Stay on your side for a minute or two before coming up slowly.

Graphic courtesy of peaceinpractice.com

2. Find 2 tennis balls, whether you are home or on the road, and place them in a sock. Make sure they stay close together in the sock – best is to push them all the way to the end of the sock. Lie down on the floor (this also works if you lie down on the bed, but you have more resistance and better alignment with the floor). Place the sock with tennis balls behind your neck, right below the bottom of your head. Relax here for about 10-15 minutes. You can even move your head side to side a bit to really feel the trigger points. This will relax your neck and shoulders. It will also help relieve tension headaches.

3. Roll you shoulders onto your back. If you were carrying a heavy bag or briefcase, or if you were slouched in the plane, your shoulders and neck probably ache. Either standing up or sitting on a chair, simply roll your shoulders onto your back. Don't shrug your shoulders up to your ears. Lift your shoulders then roll them onto your back so that you create a little shelf for your chest. Now you are in proper alignment. Whenever you feel yourself slouching or curling over your computer, roll your shoulders onto your back. This also works when you are actually carrying the heavy bag on your shoulder.

PEPPERMINT ESSENTIAL OIL:

Peppermint is the single-most versatile essential oil. It is invigorating if inhaled, calming if applied to the feet, and a digestive aid if taken internally. Traveling with Therapeutic Grade essential oils helps address many woes associated with travel. Essential oils are extremely potent and powerful, so you want to make sure they are pure–devoid of pesticides, chemicals, and artificial fillers. Look for organic and certified pure therapeutic grade essential oils in natural health food stores, neighborhood apothecaries, and online at Doterra and Young Living.

1. **CANOLA:** 90% of Canola oil in the United States is GMO. Canola oil is developed from the rapeseed plant, which is part of the mustard family of plants. These oils have long been used for industrial purposes (in candles, lipsticks, soaps, inks, lubricants, and biofuels). It is an industrial oil, not a food. The claim is that canola is safe to use because through modification it is no longer rapeseed but "canola." It was further genetically modified (GM) to resist herbicides.

2. **ASPARTAME:** An artificial sweetener, aspartame is derived from genetically modified microorganisms, found in a number of food products, especially diet soft drinks and food labeled sugar free or low sugar. It accounts for as many as 75 percent of adverse reactions to food additives reported to the Food and Drug Administration (FDA). A number of chronic illnesses have been attributed to aspartame including brain tumors, epilepsy, diabetes, birth defects, Alzheimer's and lymphoma.

3. **DAIRY:** As much as one-fifth of dairy cows in the United States today are given growth hormones to increase milk production. This figure has been rising since the FDA approved a genetically engineered recombinant bovine growth hormone known as rbGH or rbST for use in dairy cows in 1993. While said to boost production by 5-15 percent, scientists have expressed concern that the increased levels of IGF-1 (insulin growth factors-1) from hormone-treated cows may boost the risks of colon and breast cancer. In addition, factory-farm cows are generally fed GMO-based feed in the feedlots.

4. **CORN:** 80% of corn grown in the United States is genetically modified to create its own insecticide. Doctors at Sherbrooke University Hospital in Quebec recently found Bt toxin from modified corn in the blood of pregnant women and their babies, as well as in non-pregnant women. Ingredients derived from corn include: corn flour, corn gluten, corn masa, corn starch, corn syrup, cornmeal, and high fructose corn syrup (HFCS).

5. **PAPAYAS:** More than 50% of papayas grown in Hawaii since 1999 have been genetically modified to combat the Papaya Ringspot Virus. Approved for sale and consumption in the United States and Canada, GM papayas cannot be imported or sold in the European Union.

6. **POTATOES:** Potatoes have been genetically modified to fight pests, fungus, and viral diseases. Ireland has recently approved the planting of GM potatoes. The EU is on the verge of approving GM potatoes for the starch industry. GM potatoes developed by Monsanto and sold to McDonald's in the United States in 1999 were recalled. To date, GM potatoes are not commercially available for human consumption. However, the risk of cross contamination to non-GMO potato crops is of serious concern. Studies on GM potatoes have shown that mice fed GM potatoes developed weak immune systems.

7. **SOY:** 94% of soybeans grown in the United States are genetically modified to resist herbicides. Soy is included in soy flour, tofu, soy beverages, soybean oil and scores of other products, especially baked goods and pastries. Soy also goes into livestock feed. Studies have shown that hamsters fed GM soy lost their abiity to reproduce, suffered slower growth, and high mortality rates.

8. **RICE:** One of the most prevalent starches in the Asian and American diets, rice has been genetically modified to contain a high amount of vitamin A (called Golden Rice). Right now, no large scale production of genetically modified rice is taking place. Although a GM rice cultivar has been approved in the United States, farmers have not yet begun using it. An approval application for the food and feed use of LL62 rice has been submitted to the EU. It is still undergoing safety evaluations. China is mounting a public relations campaign on the safety of GM foods, which many believe is a signal that it will soon approve the commercial sale of GM rice.

9. **ZUCCHINI:** The summer squash zucchini and yellow squash have been genetically modified to resist viral and fungal disease and are available for commercial sale in the United States and Canada.

10. **SUGAR:** 95% of sugar beets grown in the United States since 2009 are genetically modified to resist Monsanto's Roundup herbicide.

11. **TOMATOES:** GMO tomatoes are no longer produced for consumption. However, tomato-based processed products such as ketchup, and tomato sauce, may have GMO-based corn syrup in them.

Salmon may become the first genetically modified animal to be approved for direct human consumption. The FDA has decided that a variety of GM salmon that grow twice as fast as their natural, un-modified peers is both safe to eat and safe for the environment.

Source:

- "Infographic unveiled: Top Ten GMO Foods to Avoid Eating", Natural News, June 5, 2012, http://www.naturalnews.com/036063_GMOs_foods_infographics.html

- GMO Compass, http://www.gmo-compass.org/eng/gmo/db/

- Institute for Responsible Technology, http://responsibletechnology.org/

- Organic Consumers Association, http://www.organicconsumers.org/

- Friends of the Earth, http://www.foe.org/projects/food-and-technology/genetic-engineering

To find out what brand name could contain GMO ingredients see the Center for Food Safety's True Food Shopper's Guide for Avoiding GMOs. http://www.centerforfoodsafety.org/fact-sheets/1974/true-food-shoppers-guide-to-avoiding-gmos

For more information on GMOs and their impact on health visit the Institute for Responsible Technology at http://responsibletechnology.org/

For more information on specific crops visit GMO Compass database. GMO Compass is a European resource set up by the European Union to monitor GMO usage. http://www.gmo-compass.org/eng/home/

II. RECOMMENDED READING:

There are many books and websites that I could recommend, but I have selected those that I think are simple, to the point, and easy to read.

→ Campbell, Colin T. and Thomas Campbell. *The China Study: Startling Implications for Diet, Weight Loss and Long-Term Health.* Texas: Benbella Books, 2006.

→ Davis, William. *Wheat Belly.* New York: Rodale, 2011.

→ Fuhrman, Joel. *Eat to Live.* New York: Little Brown and Company, 2011.

→ Fuhrman, Joel. *Nutritarian Handbook & ANDI Food Scoring Guide.* New Jersey: Gift of Health Press, 2012.

→ Gittleman, Ann Louise. *Get the Sugar Out: 501 Simple Ways to Cut the Sugar Out of Any Diet.* New York: Three Rivers Press, 2008.

→ Institute for Responsible Technology, http://responsibletechnology.org/

→ Dr. Dean Ornish http://www.ornishspectrum.com/proven-program/

→ Salatin, Joel. *Folks this aint normal.* New York: Center Street, 2011.

If you want more information, in more of a reference book format, then take a look at:

→ Cousens, Gabriel. *Conscious Eating.* California: North Atlantic Books, 2000.

If you want an excellent resource on the nutrient value of fruits, vegetables, grains, nuts and seeds take a look at:

→ Mars, Brigitte. *Rawsome.* California: Basic Health Publications, 2004.

III. RECOMMENDED VIDEOS AND DOCUMENTARIES:

✈ FoodMatters, available at http://www.foodmatters.tv/
Also available on Netflix.

✈ Forks Over Knives, available at http://www.forksoverknives.com/
Also available on Netflix.

✈ Genetic Roulette, available at http://responsibletechnology.org/

✈ Ingredients, available at http://ingredientsfilm.com/dvds.php
Also available on Netflix.

IV. MORE REFERENCES AND READING IF YOU WANT TO DIVE DEEPER:

✦ Balch, Phyllis A. *Prescription for Nutritional Healing*, 5th Ed. New York: Avery, 2010.

✦ Campbell-McBride, Dr. Natasha, *Gut and Psychology Syndrome: A Natural Treatment to Dyspraxia, Autism*, A.D.D., Dyslexia, ADHD, Depression, Schizophrenia. 2010.

✦ Challem, Jack. *The Inflammatory Syndrome: Your Nutrition Plan for Great Health, Weight Loss, and Pain Free Living.* New Jersey: John Wiley & Sons, Inc., 2010.

✦ Colquhoun, James and Laurentine Ten Bosch. *Hungry for Change: Ditch the Diets, Conquer the Cravings, and Eat Your Way to Lifelong Health.* Harper One, 2012.

✦ Cummins, Ronnie and Ben Lilliston. *Genetically Engineered Foods: A Self-Defense Guide for Consumers.* New York: Marlowe & Company, 2000.

✦ Dorfman, Kelly. *What's Eating Your Child? The Hidden Connections Between Food and Childhood Ailments.* 2011.

✦ Gerson, Charlotte with Beata Bishop. *The Gerson Way: Defeating Cancer and Other Chronic Diseases.* California: Gerson Health Media, 2010.

✦ Gittleman, Ann Louise. *The Fat Flush Plan.* New York: McGraw Hill, 2012.

✦ GMO Compass. http://www.gmo-compass.org/

✦ Hayford, Kelly. *If It's Not Food...Don't Eat It!* 2005.

✦ Katz, Sandor Elix. *The Art of Fermentation.* Vermont: Chelsea Green Publishing, 2012.

✦ O'Brien, Robyn with Rachel Kranz. *The Unhealthy Truth, One Mother's Shocking Investigation into the Dangers of America's Food Supply–And What Every Family Can Do to Protect Itself.* Harmony, 2010.

✈ Packer, Lester and Carol Colman. *The Antioxidant Miracle.* New York: John Wiley & Sons, Inc. , 1999.

✈ Pollan, Michael. *The Omnivore's Dilemma: A Natural History of Four Meals.* New York: Penguin Press, 2006.

✈ Pryor, Betsy and Sanford Holst. *Kombucha Phenomenon: The Miracle Health Tea, 2nd Edition.* Sierra Sunrise Books, 1996.

✈ Roberts, Paul. *The End of Food.* New York: Houghton Mifflin Company, 2008.

✈ Schenck, Susan and Victoria Bidwell. *The Live Food Factor: The Comprehensive Guide to the Ultimate Diet for Body, Mind, Spirit and the Planet.* 2009.

✈ The Center for Food Safety. http://www.centerforfoodsafety.org/

✈ The Organic and Non-GMO Report. http://www.non-gmoreport.com/

✈ Wolfe, David. *Superfoods: The Food and Medicine of the Future.* California: North Atlantic Books, 2009.

bio

bioavailability, 40, 44

biochemical, 31

biofuels, 91

biological, 26

Biophotonic scanner, 48; see also Antioxidant
scanner; antioxidants

biscuits, 67

bloodstream, 26

body, 1-2, 4, 10-11, 15, 19, 21-22, 25-31, 35,
37-38, 40, 44-47, 51, 53, 60, 62-64, 75-76,
88

bones, 29, 88; see also calcium

bovine growth hormone, 91

bowels, 64

box lunch, 53, 61; see also conferences

bran, 31

Brazil nuts, 66; see also nuts

bread, 41, 77; see also refined grains

breakfast, 3, 29, 56, 77, 82

breast cancer, 91

brown rice, 66

Bt toxin, 91; see also GMOs

bus, 2, 5, 70, 87

business travel, 1, 3, 13, 81

business travelers, 1; see road warriors

butter, 66; see also dairy

C

caffeine, 10, 29, 35

cakes, 29, 67

calcium, 27, 29

calories, 13, 28, 37, 74

canola, 33, 75, 91; see also GMOs

carbohydrates, 27-28

carcinogen, 30; see cancer

cellular, 22, 37, 44

Center for Food Safety, 30, 93

chai, 67, 74

chefs, 20

chocolate, 29, 39, 67

choice, 19, 23, 45, 51-53, 60, 62, 70, 73-74, 78,
81

cleanse, 10, 64-65; see also detox

coffee, 9-11, 15, 29, 49, 67, 73-74; see also
caffeine

colonics, 64; see also detox

commitment, 7, 25, 55, 62, 78, 85

conferences, 82

conscious eating, 7; see also nouri

contaminated foods, 27, 33

cookies, 29, 32, 69

corn, 28-29, 32-33, 35, 41, 52-53, 91, 93; see
also GMOs

corporate, 2, 5, 15, 56, 81-82

cost of food, 3, 14-15, 20, 32, 60, 82

cravings, 28-29

G

H

I

J

K

N

natural, 28, 39, 42-44, 56, 67, 89, 93

networking, 15, 82

neurotransmitter, 28

Non-GMO project, 42

nouri

    definition, 22, 37

    niche market, 20

    non-GMO, 38, 41-42, 49, 58, 61

    nouri, 2, 11, 20, 22-23, 29, 37-38, 40-42, 44-45, 47, 55-56, 62, 66, 69, 75, 78, 81, 85

    Nouri graph, 41

    organic, 30, 38, 42-44, 49, 51-52, 56-59, 61-62, 66-67, 74-75, 81-82, 89

    positive impact, 37

nourishing, 21

NutraSweet, 28; see also artificial sweetener

nutrientless, 28

nutrients, 11, 13, 26-29, 37-38, 40, 44, 62, 85; see also nouri

nutriment, 21

nutritarian, 94

nutrition, 15, 20; see also nouri

nutritionists, 37

nuts, 11, 39, 41, 43-44, 62, 67, 70, 73

O

oats, 39, 66

obesity, 29

oils

    bad oils, 49

    essential oils, 89

    flax oil, 38, 41

    hydrogenated oil, 33

    oil, 38, 59, 75, 89, 91-92

    olive oil, 38

    vegetable oils, 38, 73

olives, 67

optimum bio-availability, 11

optimum weight, 37, 44-45

options, 1-3, 5, 13-15, 56, 58, 63, 66-67, 69, 75, 78, 81; see also food; healthy; menu; nouri

organic certification, 42

organs, 46

overweight, 9

overwhelmed, 51

P

parasites, 59

pasta, 29, 41, 66, 75; see also grains

pasteurized, 29-30, 32, 39-40, 43-44, 64, 67, 78

pastries, 32, 41, 49, 67, 73, 92

pasture-fed, 42, 66; see also animal protein

soy; see also GMOs

    soybeans, 92

    soymilk, 74

sprouts, 39, 43, 56

starving, 73, 75

steakhouses, 81

stevia, 39, 42, 44, 61, 66; see also sweeteners

stewardess, 76

stimulants, 10, 34

stomach, 30, 75

strength, 47

stress, 1-2, 7, 10, 13, 28-29, 46-47, 63

stress management, 2

suffer, 45

sugar, 10, 13-14, 28-29, 32, 35, 37, 39, 41, 44, 48-49, 60, 66-67, 69-70, 73-76, 91, 93; see also sweeteners

sunflower seeds, 39, 43

superfoods

    avocado, 39, 41, 52

    cacao, 39

    chia seeds, 39, 41, 47, 64

    coconut, 39, 41, 43, 67

    goji berries, 39, 47

    honey, 39, 42, 44, 61, 64, 66, 70

supermarkets, 51

supplements, 3, 47, 65

sweeteners

    agave, 39, 42, 44, 61, 64, 66

    honey, 39, 42, 44, 61, 64, 66

    stevia, 39, 42, 44, 61, 66

syrup, 28-29, 32, 35, 39, 42, 44, 91, 93

T

taste, 20, 40, 52, 63-64

tea, 29, 41, 47, 49, 65, 67, 73-74

tips, 55, 70, 87

tired, 9-11, 70, 75

tofu, 32, 41, 92; see also soy

tomatoes, 11, 33, 38, 41, 52, 93; see also vegetables

tongue, 46

tortilla chips, 52-53

toxins, 10, 26, 28-29, 47, 63; see also unhealthy

transgenic, 30; see also GMOs

travel, 1, 3, 5, 13, 17, 47, 55, 69, 71, 78-79, 81-83, 87, 89

travel situations, 73-78

triglycerides, 47-48

U

unappetizing, 77

unhealthy

    birth defects, 91

    bloating, 60

    brain tumors, 91

    cancer, 30, 38, 91

    cardiovascular disease, 5, 44

    celiac disease, 5, 44

    chronic disease, 3, 18, 34, 75

    destruction of cells, 31, 35, 40

V

W

Y

Road Warrior Health Manifesto

1. Be a nouri seeker. Think nouri not food!

2. Look for flavor **and** nutrition when selecting a restaurant.

3. Be responsible for your health. Don't outsource it.

4. Avoid GMO, chemically treated, and processed foods.

5. Count nutrients, not calories.

6. Just ask yourself, is it worth the damage?

7. Turn business travel into an opportunity.

8. The world is not perfect. Go easy on yourself.

9. Enjoy the nouri experience. Enjoy your dining companions. Be well.

CPSIA information can be obtained at www.ICGtesting.com
Printed in the USA
LVOW02s1200280514

387555LV00001B/1/P